ISBN 978-0-265-11754-5
PIBN 10939630

1 MONTH OF
FREE
READING

at

www.ForgottenBooks.com

By purchasing this book you are eligible for one month membership to ForgottenBooks.com, giving you unlimited access to our entire collection of over 1,000,000 titles via our web site and mobile apps.

To claim your free month visit:

www.forgottenbooks.com/free939630

English
Français
Deutsche
Italiano
Español
Português

www.forgottenbooks.com

Mythology Photography **Fiction**
Fishing Christianity **Art** Cooking
Essays Buddhism Freemasonry
Medicine **Biology** Music **Ancient
Egypt** Evolution Carpentry Physics
Dance Geology **Mathematics** Fitness
Shakespeare **Folklore** Yoga Marketing
Confidence Immortality Biographies
Poetry **Psychology** Witchcraft
Electronics Chemistry History **Law**
Accounting **Philosophy** Anthropology
Alchemy Drama Quantum Mechanics
Atheism Sexual Health **Ancient History**
Entrepreneurship Languages Sport
Paleontology Needlework Islam
Metaphysics Investment Archaeology
Parenting Statistics Criminology
Motivational

REPORT OF THE COMMISSIONERS

ON

Proposals for Sites & Plans for Buildings

FOR THE

Deaf and Dumb, the Blind, and the Feeble-Minded,

IN THE

STATE OF NEW JERSEY,

For the Year 1874-5.

NEWARK, N. J.:

NEWARK DAILY JOURNAL—W. B. GUILD, BOOK AND JOB PRINTER.

1875.

REPORT OF THE COMMISSIONERS

ON

Proposals for Sites & Plans for Buildings

FOR THE

Deaf and Dumb, the Blind, and the Feeble-Minded,

IN THE

STATE OF NEW JERSEY,

For the Year 1874-5.

NEWARK, N. J.:

NEWARK DAILY JOURNAL—W. B. GUILD, BOOK AND JOB PRINTER.

1875.

IV15A75

ACT FORMING COMMISSION.

An Act to Provide for the Education of the Deaf and Dumb, the Blind, and the Feeble-Minded in this State.

WHEREAS, the commissioners heretofore appointed by the governor have reported that there exists at present, within the state, no schools adequate for imparting education to the pupils who are either deaf and dumb, blind, or feeble-minded, and that there are, at the present time, at least one hundred and fifty deaf and dumb, one hundred blind, and one hundred feeble-minded pupils who would gladly avail themselves of such facilities as the state might provide ; *and whereas,* it is the duty of the state to educate these, her unfortunate children ;

1. BE IT ENACTED, *by the Senate and General Assembly of the State of New Jersey,* That Charles D. Deshler, Jeremiah Baker, William S. Yard, Charles D. Hendrickson, Ralph B. Gowdy, and Eldridge Mix be, and they are hereby appointed commissioners to advertise for and receive proposals for sites, that is to say, for a site upon which to erect suitable buildings in which to board and instruct pupils who are deaf and dumb, which site shall contain not less than twenty acres of ground ; for a site upon which to erect suitable buildings in which to board and educate pupils who are blind, which site shall contain not less than five acres of ground ; for a site upon which to erect suitable buildings in which to board and educate pupils who are feeble-minded, which site shall contain not less than fifty acres ; that all these sites shall be remote from malarial influences, capable of complete drainage and of securing thereon an abundant supply of sweet, soft water ; which proposals shall name the lowest price at which the land will be sold to the state—giving to the state an option to purchase the same, at the price named, at any time before the first day of April, eighteen hundred and seventy-five.

2. *And be it enacted,* That said commissioners may procure from competent experts plans for the several buildings in which may be boarded and educated one hundred and fifty deaf and dumb pupils, one hundred blind, and one hundred feeble-minded, with all con-

venient and proper appliances for their comfort, instruction, and preservation of health; and for the accommodation of the officers, teachers, and assistants; which buildings shall be, when constructed, of durable material, and shall be limited in cost as follows: that for the deaf and dumb not to exceed one hundred and fifty thousand dollars; that for the blind not to exceed one hundred thousand dollars; and that for the feeble-minded not to exceed eighty thousand dollars.

3. *And be it enacted*, That the said commissioners shall report, with their opinions thereon, the proposals and plans they may receive under this act to the governor, to be by him laid before the next legislature.

4. *And be it enacted*, That to defray the entire expenses which the said commissioners may incur under this act, the sum of two thousand dollars is hereby appropriated, to be drawn from the treasury only upon proper detailed vouchers, signed by the commissioners, and audited and certified by the comptroller.

Approved March 27, 1874.

REPORT.

To His Excellency Joseph D. Bedle, Governor of the State of New Jersey:

SIR: The undersigned, commissioners appointed by an act of the legislature of 1874, entitled "An act to provide for the education of the deaf and dumb, the blind, and the feeble-minded, in this State," approved March 27th, 1874, (a copy of which is hereto annexed,) respectfully submit the following report:

The honor in the State of New Jersey of the *first step* in the humane inquiry, which has for its object the adequate care and education of the unfortunate classes above named, is due to the legislature of 1873, which, in response to a petition of the Synod of New Jersey, of the Presbyterian Church, asking that "immediate action be taken for the founding and proper administration of an asylum for the benefit of deaf mutes," passed an act, approved March 11th, 1873, entitled "An act for the appointment of commissioners to examine into the condition," not only of deaf mutes, but of "the deaf and dumb, blind, and feeble-minded inhabitants of this State."

The report of the commissioners appointed by virtue of this last mentioned act was made to the legislature of 1874, and embraced the following particulars: (1) the condition of these classes in this State; (2) their number; (3) the feasibility of building an institution or institutions for them; and (4) the bringing together in a compact view a large mass of information, derived from persons of great experience engaged in the care and education of these classes, comprising particulars as to the co-education of the deaf and dumb, the blind, and the feeble-minded, or any of them; the requisites for for sites for institutions intended for them; the cost of constructing the necessary buildings, and of the maintenance of their inmates; and much other matter of permanent value bearing upon the whole subject committed by the legislature to the commissioners for investigation. The report stated that the condition of these unfortunates in our State was deplorable, and that their whole number was certainly not less than 2,100, and probably exceeded 2,600; but recognizing the certainty that the people of the State might be unable or unwilling to provide *asylums* for the whole of this large body, and for other reasons which they recited, the commissioners recommended that instead of *asylums* for the custody and maintenance of all the defectives without regard to age or improvability, the State should inaugurate a *system of schools* for the education and training of so many of them, within the educable ages and susceptible of education, as might be ready to avail of the same; which schools, they suggested, would be the legitimate complement of our system of public schools, and should be as free to the afflicted classes as our common schools are to the unafflicted. The commissioners concluded their report by expressing the conviction—based upon a careful and prolonged canvass—that at least 150 deaf and dumb, 100 blind, and 100 feeble-minded, all of the educable class, are now ready and desirous to enter such institutions, if provided by the State; and by recommending that, " on this basis, steps be taken to erect three separate institutions, the buildings to be so planned as that they may be easily enlarged from time to time, as our needs may require."

The act under which the present commissioners were appointed, was the *second step* of the State of New Jersey in this honorable and enlightened inquiry; and its preamble, accepting the undeniable statement of the former commissioners that " there exists at present within the State no schools adequate for imparting education to pupils who are deaf and dumb, blind, or feeble-minded," notwithstanding that there are at the present time at least 350 of these several classes " who would gladly avail themselves of such facilities as the State might provide," placed on record the grave declaration of the legislature of 1874, that " IT IS THE DUTY OF THE STATE TO EDUCATE HER UNFORTUNATE CHILDREN"—a declaration which, we trust, no subsequent legislature of the State of New Jersey will be willing to repudiate or reverse.

The duties which were imposed upon the undersigned commissioners, by the act appointing them, were as follows:

1. To advertise for and receive proposals for three separate sites, respectively, of not less than twenty acres, five acres, and fifty acres, on which to erect buildings in which to board and instruct pupils who are deaf and dumb, blind, and feeble-minded.

2. To procure from competent experts plans for the several buildings, of durable material, in which may be boarded and educated 150 deaf and dumb, 100 blind, and 100 feeble-minded pupils, with all convenient and proper appliances for their comfort, instruction, and preservation of health, and for the accommodation of the necessary officers, teachers, and assistants.

3. To report the said proposals and plans, with their opinions thereon, to the Governor.

Although the act appointing the commissioners was promptly approved by your predecessor, on the 27th of March, 1874, yet, from the inadvertent omission of a proviso making it take effect immediately, it did not go into operation until July 4th, 1874, thereby shortening by more than three months the time allotted to the commissioners for the performance of the duties confided to them. These duties proved so large and various, and required so great an amount of time for correspondence and conferences with experts; for the examination and perfection of plans; for the advertisement and reception of proposals, and for the visitation and inspection of the sites offered, that the completion of the work committed to their charge, notwithstanding the utmost diligence, has been impossible at an earlier date than the present; and for these reasons their report, also, has been necessarily deferred. .

CONCERNING SITES.

In conformity with the requirements of the act, proposals for sites were advertised in two or more papers in each county in the State; and in response a large number of proposals were received, coming from parties resident in sixteen different counties. All the sites, thus offered, which combined the requisites prescribed by the act, have been visited either by the commissioners in a body, or by committees appointed from among their number, and have been carefully inspected with reference to their exposure to or freedom from malarial influences, their susceptibility to complete drainage, and their command of an abundant supply of sweet soft water. All these proposals are herewith submitted to your Excellency.

When considering this large mass of proposals, the commissioners supposed that it was not the design or the desire of the legislature to have each separate site described and reported upon in detail, as to its relative or intrinsic advantages or disadvantages. They have, therefore, proceeded upon the idea that, in giving their opinion upon them, as required by the act, they should confine their report specifically to those only which most completely of any embody the needs and requirements of the institutions proposed to be built upon them. Proceeding upon this construction, from the numerous sites offered and inspected, they have made a selection of the one, for each institution, which pre-eminently combines all the conditions prescribed in the act, and that are considered essential by experts of acknowledged intelligence and experience in their several specialties.

By referring to the report of the commissioners to the legislature of 1874, it will be perceived that among other questions one asking specific information as to the requisites needed for sites, was addressed to twenty-seven superintendents and teachers of institutions charged with the care of the classes of unfortunates in whose interest the present inquiry is conducted. In the replies received from these gentlemen, there was entire unanimity upon the following particulars: That all these institutions should be in a rolling or undulating country, free from malarial influences, sufficiently elevated for sewerage and drainage, near an ample supply of water, cleared and exposed to the sun and air, and having some woodland. That institutions for the deaf and dumb, and for the blind, should be in or near a large town or city, because of the advantages thereby afforded for procuring supplies and servants, and for the sale of the products of the industrial departments; and also because of the indispensable educational advantages to be derived from lectures, concerts, churches, manufactures, stores, street sights, and social influences and surroundings. That institutions for the feeble-minded should be in the country, but convenient of access to and from a town or city.

In their consideration of the sites offered to them, the commissioners have held themselves strictly to the conditions laid down and recommended with such great unanimity by the experienced instructors whom they had consulted. It is proper to add that, in canvassing the merits of the sites offered, the commissioners also considered accessibility to the bulk of the population of the state to be a highly desirable element, though not absolutely indispensable.

SITE FOR INSTITUTION FOR DEAF AND DUMB.

Among the proposals sent in to the commissioners, were six from a committee of the Board of Aldermen of the city of New Brunswick, in conformity with a resolution of that body, passed August 24th, 1874, and which was unanimously ratified by a largely attended public meeting of the citizens and tax-payers, called for the consideration of the subject, and presided over by the mayor of the city, August 31st, 1874. These proposals offered to present to the state any one of the six sites therein described, that should be deemed the most suitable, as a gift, free from all municipal assessments and taxes, on condition that the state would erect thereon an institution for the deaf and dumb. These sites—all of which were found to be desirable—were visited and inspected by the commissioners, on several occasions, between September 1st and October 22d last past, comprising the period of the severe drouth of last autumn; and, during the same interval, they were diligently engaged in visiting and examining, with special reference to an institution for the deaf and dumb, a number of other sites that had been offered in various parts of the state. After a deliberate and exhaustive examination and comparison of all the sites offered which were in any degree suitable for such an institution, the commissioners unanimously agreed that the site which combined, not only more numerous advantages than any other, but which possessed, in an eminent degree, all the requisites that were desired, was a tract offered by the city of New Brunswick, lying in the southerly part of the city, in the First ward, on the high bank of the Raritan, back of Sonman's Hill, consisting of forty-three acres and a fraction, and composed as follows: thirty-two and a-half acres, comprising part of Riverside Grove, belonging to A. D. Newell; five and a-half acres, adjoining the above on the east, belonging to J. C. Carpender; and five and a-half acres adjoining the above on the west, belonging to James Hurley—the cost to the city of the entire tract being $31,790. This tract lies between Burnet street on the east, and Clifton avenue on the west, and has a front of over thirteen hundred feet on the former, and nearly a thousand feet on the latter. It is about one hundred feet above the level of the Raritan river, and on the Burnet street front is five hundred feet distant from it. The plot is beautifully undulating, and is diversified with ravines, vales, and upland. It is in a fine state of cultivation; has an abundant water supply, both natural and artificial; and is enriched by noble growths of lofty forest trees, disposed at various points, where they are likely to be the most needful or desirable. So far as the commissioners were able to discover, there was nothing lacking in the site, either on the score of health, beauty, utility, or exact adaptedness to the needs of an institution for the deaf and dumb. These impressions of the commissioners have been since confirmed by experts who were invited to visit the site, and consulted as to its suitableness. One of the most distinguished and experienced of these, the superintendent, for many years, of a large and successful institution in a sister state, addressed the following note on the subject, to the chairman of the commission:

"Since my very pleasant visit to your city, the beautiful site, so generously donated for the uses of a deaf and dumb institution by your corporate authorities, has been frequently in my mind, and I have felt moved to write to you, congratulating your commission upon their good fortune in securing this very desirable site. Such a site for such an institution, would be cheap to the state, at any price. I regard it one of the most eligible situations that I have ever seen anywhere; and am unable to recall any important requisite for such an institution that it does not possess. Its proximity to New Brunswick; its easy accessibility to New York, on the one hand, and Philadelphia on the other, with its natural diversity of surface, accompanied with a charming and extensive prospect, all combine to fill the entire demands of the site of an institution for the education of the deaf and dumb. No institution in the country has a more favorable situation than yours will have."

In addition to the advantages above recited, the citizens of New Brunswick have secured from the Delaware and Raritan Canal

Company the privilege of a free dock on the bank of the Raritan, in front of the property, on which to erect a boat-house, whence the pupils will have access to the Raritan, out of the way of passing boats, where they may have a safe and uninterrupted course for physical exercise with the oar, on a sheet of water over a mile in length. This is considered a most valuable acquisition, indispenable to the health and vigor of the pupils, and ministering largely to their enjoyment.

The commissioners had, therefore, no hesitation in arriving at a unanimous determination to recommend the acceptance by the State of the above named site, on the conditions stated in the proposal, for the purposes of an institution for the deaf and dumb; and on the 24th of October last advised the committee of the Common Council of New Brunswick to that effect. In response to the communication of the commissioners, the committee of Common Council, under date of November 10th, 1874, wrote that they had consummated a contract with the owners of the land indicated, by which, on that day, the several owners had executed to the municipality full title-deeds for the property, to be held in escrow pending the ratification of the selection made by the commissioners by the legislature, on which ratification the city is in turn pledged to convey the said property to the State.

The commissioners earnestly recommend the legislature to accept the gift of this beautiful, convenient, and valuable site, and to take such legislative action as may be necessary to enable the citizens of New Brunswick to carry their generous proffer into effect.

SITE FOR INSTITUTION FOR THE BLIND.

At an early day, when considering the subject of a site for an institution for the blind, the question of the adaptability for that use of the "Soldiers' Children's Home," in the vicinity of Trenton, presented itself to the attention of the commissioners. That institution belongs to the State, which has invested in the grounds, buildings, and improvements the sum of $69,000. The act originating the "Home" as a State institution and making an appropriation for its construction, was passed March 7th, 1866, and contemplated the termination of its use for present purposes in ten years from that date, as did also the act of April 1st, 1869, appropriating two thousand dollars per year "for seven successive years" from the last mentioned date, to pay the wages of teachers, etc. Both these acts, and the original application for its establishment, estimated the period of the existence of the "Home" at ten years, and assumed that it would terminate in 1876. Whether this expectation will be realized, we are unable to foretell. In their last report the managers of the Home state that " the number of children is now materially diminished; the average number, from being at one time two hundred and twenty, is now one hundred and fifty-three "—of whom, we may add, one hundred and eight are derived from six counties only, the remaining forty-five being drawn from the fifteen other counties of the State. The " Home " reached its maximum in 1870, at the close of which the number of children remaining in it was two hundred and twenty ; at the close of 1871 the number was reduced to two hundred and nine ; in 1872, to one hundred and ninety-five; and at the present time to one hundred and fifty. As a residence in the " Home " terminates upon the children attaining the age of fifteen, and as there are scarcely any new admissions to it, (none are reported by the managers for the past year,) there can be little doubt that, even if the legislature should decide to extend its existence for a time, the institution will expire from natural causes in the course of a very few years. The commissioners would deplore the use of any means to hasten this result, and trust the state will continue its fostering care and protection of the children of our soldiers as long as they are needed. Yet we have felt it to be our duty not to ignore the not distant event of the close of the " Home." The commissioners, therefore, employed an architect to examine the buildings with a view to their utilization as a part of an institution for the blind ; and finding that this was feasible, they had plans prepared, embodying the necessary alterations and additions, which will be more fully referred to elsewhere in this report. They came the more readily to this conclusion, since the site—which consists of seven acres of land, upon two of which is a fine grove—is amply sufficient for the needs of an institution for the blind, and is delightfully situated in a healthy and airy location, about fifteen minutes' walk from the railroad station in Trenton. No more desirable site for such an institution has been brought to the notice of the commissioners, and they recommend that as soon as, in the opinion of the legislature, the present objects of the " Home" shall have been accomplished, it shall be applied to the uses of an institution for the blind, in conformity with the plans hereinafter described.

SITE FOR AN INSTITUTION FOR THE FEEBLE-MINDED.

After a long and careful examination and survey of a large number of sites in different parts of the state, with special reference to an institution for the feeble-minded, the commissioners have unanimously arrived at the conclusion that the one which combines more fully than any other all the needs and requirements of such an institution, is a tract of land about three-quarters of a mile from Bordentown, extending from Ward avenue on the south to the Public road from Bordentown to Crosswicks on the north, having a front on each of over two thousand feet, and consisting of one hundred and twenty-five acres, the property of William S. Herbert, and of twenty-five acres, the property of Antone Kline—being one hundred and fifty acres in all. The tract is cut up into fields of ten acres, and is a parallelogram; the soil is excellent, and in a fine state of cultivation; on the property is a pear nursery of five hundred trees, a peach orchard of one thousand trees, and an apple orchard of six acres, all in full bearing; besides a conservatory of plants and flowers. The farm houses, which comprise a comfortable dwelling house for a farmer, capacious barns, stable, and outhouses, are in excellent condition, and are located precisely where they will be needed, on the northerly portion of the tract. The fencing is exceptionally good. The site is one mile from the Delaware river, a short distance from the well known Joseph Bonaparte grounds, and has an elevation of one hundred and ninety feet above tide water of the Delaware—affording a fine and extensive prospect for many miles on every side. It is capable of complete drainage, either into the Delaware or Crosswicks Creek; and the right of way for such drainage is guaranteed to the state in writing. The land composing the site slopes gradually from the fronts on Ward avenue and on the Public road to Crosswicks, to a point very nearly in the centre of the tract, where the property is traversed from east to west by an abundant and never-failing stream of pure soft water, fed from living springs, from which it was formerly proposed to supply the city of Bordentown with water; and from ponds fed by which the city now obtains its annual supply of ice. The commissioners have secured from the owners of the several properties, on which the springs have their rise that are the sources of this stream, and through which it passes before reaching the tract, a guarantee in writing, herewith presented, that the said stream shall not be diverted, contaminated by any means, or lessened in volume, and engaging to execute papers which shall secure these conditions to the state. The portion of the tract most eligible for the buildings for an institution fronts on Ward avenue, being on the summit of the slope opposite to and sufficiently remote from the farm buildings, which are on the summit of the slope fronting on the Public road to Crosswicks. The portion of the property lying on the last named road is about three hundred yards from the branch railroad from Bordentown to Amboy; and a number of wealthy and influential citizens of Bordentown have entered into an engagement in writing, which is herewith submitted, to build a switch from the railroad to the site at this point, which will be of great and permanent value to the State for the transportation of building materials, coal, and supplies for the institution. There is an abundance of gravel and of good brick clay on the place.

The size of the tract is larger than the minimum named in the act—"not less than fifty acres"—but it is not larger than will be advantageous, and even necessary, since the chief and almost the sole occupation to which the feeble-minded can be trained, and the one which is absolutely essential to their physical well-being, is out-of-door farm work. While they are being indurated in health, and trained to habits of self-support, as cultivation of the soil, they will, at the same time, become contributors to the food supply of the institution, and thus materially lessen its current annual expenses. Finally, the tract is situated in an elevated and salubrious locality ; is surrounded by a rolling country, is susceptible of perfect drainage into tide-water streams, and combines every advantage of being in the country, though adjacent to a city, together with easy and frequent means of communication to and from all parts of the state.

The cost of the entire tract of one hundred and fifty acres, as above described, is $18,500, with the option to the state at that price till April 1st, 1875. The commissioners unanimously and earnestly recommend the legislature to secure this eminently appropriate site, at the price, on the conditions, and with the guarantees above recited.

PLANS FOR BUILDINGS.

The provision of the act making it the duty of the commissioners to procure from " competent experts" plans for the several buildings required for the care and education of the classes specified in the act, was prompted by practical good sense. No mere architect, however accomplished, could understand the complex and peculiar needs of such institutions, in all their infinity of detail and with reference to their administrative, educational, and industrial requirements. None but experienced specialists could be experimentally familiar with the diversified requisites essential to the comfort, convenience, and efficient instruction of the peculiarly exceptional classes for whom such institutions are designed. Not even the specialist whose life has been devoted to the observation and instruction of the deaf and dumb, could be safely entrusted with the designing of an institution for the blind or the feeble-minded. And the converse is equally true. The characters of the several classes of defectives; the modes of instruction ; the nature of the defect to be remedied, alleviated, or substituted for—these, and many other features, are essentially, and, in some respects, diametrically diverse. Information, to be valuable, must be derived, in each branch, almost exclusively from those who are most intimately acquainted with all its needs and requirements.

Acting upon this judicious provision, immediately upon the act going into effect, the commissioners addressed the leading educators of the deaf and dumb, the blind, and the feeble-minded in the United States and England, requesting each, in his several specialty, to furnish outlines, ground-plans, etc., of the proposed institutions, which should combine the results of the most advanced experience, and cover all the requisites for the comfort, health, and instruction of the pupils, together with accommodations for the officers, teach-

ers, and assistants—the whole to be drawn to a scale, and the
several parts and details so denoted as that non-specialists might
readily comprehend them, or an architect use them as a guide in
preparing his working plans. In response to these requests, plans
were received from a large number of gentlemen, tracings of which
were made and interchanged among them for examination, criti-
cism, revision, or amendment, with the object in view of securing
such a "harmony" of the various plans upon essential particulars
as would at once embody the results of the largest and most
approved experience, and protect the State from the perpetuation
of venerable errors. For their prompt and cordial responses to our
appeal for plans and information, for the active interest they have
taken in the inquiry, for the sacrifice of time and liberal contributions of labor, and for their disinterested assistance, the commissioners feel under special obligations, which they take this opportu-
nity gratefully to acknowledge, to the following distinguished
educators: E. M. Gallandet, LL. D., of Washington, D. C.; Wm.
H. Churchman, M. A., Indianapolis, Ind.; Isaac L. Peet, LL. D.,
New York city; Philip G. Gillett, LL. D., Jacksonville, Ill.; Dr.
Asa D. Lord, Batavia, N. Y.; Mr. G. O. Fay, Columbus, O.; Isaac
N. Kerlin, M. D., Media, Pa.; Mr. Von Praagh, London, England;
Mr. William B. Wait, New York city; Mr. J. A. McWhorter,
Baton Rouge, La.; W. D. Williams, M. A., Macon, Ga.; Mr.
Thomas H. Little, Janesville, Wis.; Mr. Thomas McIntire, Jack-
sonville, Ill.; Mr. John D. Parker, Wyandotte, Kansas; Joshua
Rhoads, M. D., Jacksonville, Ill.; Mr. J. L. Noyes, Faribault,
Minn. ; and Mr. Egbert L. Bangs, Flint, Mich.

The product of the prolonged inquiry of the commissioners, after
a subsequent study and comparison of all the plans in the light of
the criticisms, alterations, and improvements suggested by the
experts consulted, is the accompanying perfected outline plans,
marked respectively, "Plan for an Institution for the Deaf and
Dumb," "Plan for an Institution for the Blind," and "Plan for an
Institution for the Feeble-Minded." It will be perceived that these
plans are not elaborated by an architect in all the minutiæ of their
details, as if intended for working plans. Even if such plans had
been considered desirable, their cost would have been an insupera-
ble obstacle in the way of procuring them, in view of the limited
amount of the appropriation at the command of the commissioners,
the whole amount of which ($2,000) would have been barely suffi-
cient for a single plan on such a scale. But they were not deemed
necessary at this stage; and the plans presented are rather intended
as an important contribution of information, embodying essential
guiding principles and ideas as to the interior disposition and
arrangements of the several institutions, which will be invaluable
aids when preparing the more elaborate working plans.

The several plans—of which full drawings have been made by

an architect, Mr. Augustus Eichorn, of Orange—are more particularly described as follows:

PLAN OF INSTITUTION FOR THE DEAF AND DUMB.

The building is cruciform, with lateral wings; three stories in height, with a cellar underneath the whole. In the rear of the centre building is a boiler and engine house. The entire front including the wings, is three hundred and twenty feet, and its depth, excluding boiler and engine house, is one hundred and seventy-four feet. Though it may be built either of stone or brick, the drawings indicate stone as the material of the structure. The style of architecture is the English Gothic, which is much in use in England for buildings of this character. Each story is arranged for the accommodation of a separate grade of pupils, classified according to their ages and advancement. Thus: the first story is designed for the sleeping and school rooms of those in the primary department; the second story, for those in the intermediate department; and the third story for the higher classes of advanced pupils. The centre buildings, both front and rear, contain rooms for the officers and teachers; and also those needed for the uses of all the pupils in common, such as an assembly room, school rooms, dining hall, library, museum, etc. But provision is made for the complete separation of the sexes, in respect to sitting rooms, play rooms, sleeping apartments, etc. The building will accommodate one hundred and eighty pupils (or even two hundred, if necessary,) besides officers, teachers and servants. The plan contemplates an increase of its capacity, so as to accommodate one hundred more than the above number, by the addition of lateral or transverse wings, as they may be required.

The following are some of the main features of the building, as set forth in the plan: (1) The rooms devoted to educational purposes are grouped in the centre and are in the front, occupying the most prominent part of the edifice, at the point of its chiefest dignity; while the dormitories are in the extreme wings for the most part, so arranged as to enjoy on all sides the most thorough exposure to the air and sunlight. (2) Provision is made for the complete separation of the sexes, except when they are under the immediate supervision of an officer or teacher. (3) The servants' department is so arranged as to secure an entire separation of the pupils from all contact with the employees in that department, and to prevent their association with them. (4) Ample provision is made for thorough ventilation and heating, for drainage, and for protection from fire. (5) Unusual facilities are afforded for the proper grading and classification of the pupils according to age and the state of their advancement in their studies. (6) While its style of architecture is simple, and its manner of construction plain and substantial, its proportions are so distributed, and its different parts so adjusted to each other, as to make the general effect tasteful and imposing.

The maximum cost of the building, at the present prices for labor and materials, according to the careful estimates of reliable builders, will be $180,000.

PLAN OF INSTITUTION FOR THE BLIND.

The plan submitted embodies the building now used for the Soldiers' Children's Home, and contemplates additional buildings in the centre, extending to the front and rear, making the structure cruciform, with transverse wings. It will be three stories in height, with a basement underneath the whole building; and will have a front of two hundred and four feet, (the present front of the Soldiers' Children's Home,) and a depth of two hundred and forty-seven feet. The architecture will be in keeping with the part to be retained, and will incline to the pointed or Gothic style. The basement floor is intended for work-rooms, play-rooms, bath-rooms, and laundry purposes. The first floor comprises rooms and offices for the superintendent and others associated with him in the management of the institution, work and play rooms for the different sexes, dining hall, gymnasium, kitchen, etc. The second story is almost wholly devoted to the educational department, and comprises class rooms, piano rooms, sewing rooms, and the private apartments of the superintendent. The third story has an assembly room in the centre building; and the remainder is principally devoted to dormitories for pupils and teachers, and hospitals for both sexes, with the necessary appurtenances. Ample provision is made in the several parts of the building for speedy and easy exit in case of fire. It is proposed to be heated by steam, and ventilated by flues built into the walls in the inner part of the building. In order to do this, the inner walls of the present edifice must be built anew, as they are now wooden partitions merely.

The aim of the commissioners in these alterations has been, to use the materials in the present structure to the best advantage compatible with the needs of an institution for the blind; to make the additions in the centre of such a character, and so ample in their dimensions, that lateral wings might be added, and the accommodations for additional pupils be afforded, as the necessity demands, without necessitating any changes in the central and main portion of the building; to adapt the building in every way to the special needs and requirements of the blind pupils whom it is designed to educate, so that their care and instruction may be conducted in the most systematic and satisfactory manner.

The cost of the alterations and additions proposed, at the present prices of labor and materials, as estimated by builders, will be

$110,000; and it will accommodate one hundred and forty, or, if need be, one hundred and fifty pupils.

PLAN OF INSTITUTION FOR THE FEEBLE-MINDED.

The building for this institution, when ultimately finished as per the plan presented herewith, will be three hundred and twenty feet in length, and two hundred and twenty-seven feet in depth. It will be cruciform, consisting of a main central edifice, with transverse wings; and will be built of brick, faced on the front and sides with Trenton brick. It will have a basement entirely above ground, and two upper stories. The basement will be eleven feet high, and will contain a dining hall, kitchen, work-rooms, etc. The principal or first story will be fourteen feet high, and will contain public rooms and offices, together with dormitories and school rooms. The third story will be devoted to the private rooms of the superintendent, dormitories, and teachers' rooms. Fewer rooms for educational purposes are needed for this class of unfortunates than for the deaf and dumb and the blind; but there must be ample provision for their physical care and training. It is not proposed by the commissioners that the whole building exhibited in the plan submitted shall be erected at present, but merely the centre portion and one wing, as indicated by the shaded drawings. The other wing can be added when additional accommodations shall be needed, when the building will present a symmetrical appearance, and its parts will be harmonious. For the present, and perhaps for years to come, the first story can be used for one sex, and the second story for the other. The portion of the building now proposed to be constructed, will accommodate one hundred and ten pupils, besides officers and teachers. The estimated cost of the whole building, when completed as planned, is $200,000, and it will accommodate two hundred and twenty pupils. But the portion designated by the shaded drawings, and which is all that is now needed, can be erected of plain and substantial materials for $125,000.

The plans followed in preparing the drawings for this institution were furnished to the commissioners, for whom they were expressly prepared, by Isaac N. Kirlin, M. D., the capable superintendent of the Pennsylvania Training School for Feeble-Minded Children, at Media, Pennsylvania, who ranks among the most experienced and distinguished of the educators of this class of unfortunates in the United States. The commissioners have not thought it desirable to depart materially from the plan with which he has favored us, and which comprises the results of many years of experience and observation.

2

REMARKS.

It will be perceived that all the buildings proposed in the plans submitted are cruciform in shape. The almost universal testimony of experts is in favor of this form as preferable to any other for buildings on the pile system, on the score that it is more completely open on all sides to air and sunlight, and is free from the chilly, shady, damp, and cheerless courts, which are inseparable from the quadrangular or other angular forms of buildings, and have proven unfavorable to the health of their inmates. Sun and air are especially needed for defectives of all kinds, because of their tendency to strumous or scrofulous diseases. A cruciform building, properly placed, will be reached by the rays of the sun in all its parts in the course of every day, and is exposed on every side at all times to the purifying and invigorating action of the air.

It will also not escape notice that the estimated cost and capacity of the several buildings are somewhat in excess of the limitation prescribed in the act. The act prescribed that the institution for the deaf and dumb should accommodate one hundred and fifty pupils, and should cost not to exceed $150,000 ; that the institution for the blind should accommodate one hundred pupils, and should cost not to exceed $100,000 ; and that the one for the feeble-minded should accommodate one hundred pupils, and should cost not to exceed $80,000. On the other hand, the plans presented are for an institution for the deaf and dumb to accommodate one hundred and eighty pupils, and to cost $180,000; for an institution for the blind to accommodate one hundred and forty pupils, and to cost $110,000; and for an institution for the feeble-minded to accommodate one hundred and ten pupils, and to cost $125,000. The departure from the limitation has been enforced by unavoidable architectural necessities, growing out of the educational and other requirements of the several institutions, the provision for which must be the same, in many respects, for an institution of either fifty, one hundred, or two hundred pupils. Each needs the same amount of space for the accommodation of the superintendent, matron, steward, and other permanent officers. Each must have an assembly room, a dining hall, a kitchen, and laundry, and rooms for a museum, a library, and for hospitals, and a dispensary. Though the institutions may require to be enlarged for additional pupils, as the State increases in population, under the plans presented such enlargement is practicable at a comparatively slight cost ; but no enlargement of the educational or administrative departments will be needed for many years, even with a largely increased number of inmates. The commissioners found as they proceeded with the plans, that a literal adherence to the limitation of the act in respect to the number of pupils and the cost of construction would involve a sacrifice of indispensable requisites, defeat the important object of thoroughly adapting the buildings for the uses for which they are intended, and would entail at an early day costly and perhaps injurious alterations. It would have been convenient to ignore these considerations and to have underestimated the outlay required, but it would have been deceitful and dishonest to have done so; and therefore, the commissioners have frankly presented estimates which they believe to be strictly fair, and in each case excessive rather than the reverse. The estimate of the commissioners in their report of last year, which estimate was based upon the average cost of such institutions in the various States, was that plain and substantial buildings for the deaf and dumb, and the blind, would cost $1,000 per pupil, and a similar building for the feeble-minded would cost $800 per pupil. According to the plans now submitted, the cost of the buildings, based on careful and detailed estimates by a reliable architect, approximates very closely to the above figures; that for the deaf and dumb being $1,000 per pupil, that for the blind $786 per pupil, and that for the feeble-minded, when the building shall be ultimately completed according to the plans, $909 per pupil.

In submitting these plans to your Excellency and the legislature, the commissioners do not desire to be understood as conveying the impression that they are not susceptible of further improvement. While we are persuaded that the governing general principles of the several plans will stand the test of severe scrutiny, and need not be materially departed from, we are conscious that continued inquiry and investigation may reveal the desirability of changes or modifications of some of the details. On this account, it would be a great misfortune to bind any trustees, whom the legislature may hereafter entrust with the construction of either or all the institutions in question, to a literal adherence to the plans now submitted. They are presented by the commissioners as so much valuable practical information, gathered from persons of unusual experience in their several specialties, and reduced to form. We, therefore, respectfully recommend that a liberal discretion be permitted as to the details of the several plans.

EXPENSES OF THE COMMISSION.

The amount appropriated "to defray the entire expenses" which the commissioners should incur, was two thousand dollars. In rendering a statement of their expenditures, the commissioners take occasion to say that they have not retained from the sum appropriated, any compensation for their services, nor would they accept it. The many days, and the prolonged thought and labor they have given during two successive years to the unsought duties imposed upon them, are their contributions as citizens, toward the payment of the debt which the State owes to those of its helpless classes who are made so by the visitation of God, and not by any agency of their own.

The following is a statement of our expenditures, which have been paid by the comptroller:

Amount of the appropriation,		$2,000 00
Paid for advertising,	$271 85	
" " printing,	127 50	
" experts for plans,	250 00	
" architect for drawings,	623 50	
" Secretary of State for certified copy of act	2 00	
" commissioners for moneys advanced for railroad fares, hotel expenses, conveyances to visit sites, postage, expressage, stationery, tracing paper, telegrams, etc.,	383 53	
		1,658 38
Balance unexpended,		$341 62

REFLECTIONS, RECOMMENDATIONS, ETC.

Before closing their report, the commissioners venture to present to the consideration of your Excellency and the legislature, some reflections and recommendations which are germain to the inquiry that has been committed to them.

In the earlier part of this report, the commissioners recommended the purchase by the State of a single site, namely, that intended for an institution for the feeble-minded. This is the only expenditure for a site that will be required, if the legislature accepts the desirable tract offered gratuitously by the city of New Brunswick for an institution for the deaf and dumb; and if it adopts the recommendation to convert the "Soldiers' Children's Home," at Trenton, into an institution for the blind. The total outlay required for sites for the three proposed institutions is, therefore, reduced to the moderate sum of $18,500.

If the recommendation of the commissioners to convert the "Soldiers' Children's Home" to the uses of an institution for the blind, and the consequent temporary postponement of the establishment of the latter, is adopted by the legislature, the immediate provision required to be made for the care and education of our defective classes is reduced to an institution for the deaf and dumb, and an institution for the feeble-minded. If a due regard be paid to frugality of expenditure, and if just views govern as to the proper character of these public buildings, it is believed that they can be erected for the amount specified in this report under the head of "plans for building," or for a gross sum not materially in excess thereof. For many reasons, chief among which are their superior durability, and the security of their young and helpless inmates from fire, the buildings should be of brick or stone, and fire-proof. But splendid or elaborate architectural finish, or a profusion of costly exterior or interior ornamentation would be superfluous elegancies. The first thing to consider, as was once wisely and wittily said by Sydney Smith is, " what it is most *needful* to have, what it is most *shameful* to want—shirts and stockings, before frills and collars." Our afflicted classes bitterly need and piteously appeal for essentials, not luxuries; and these, we believe, it is within the ability of this prosperous and wealthy State to supply. There should be no unnecessary embellishments or lavish adornments in public institutions of this kind; but they should be the most inexpensive buildings possible consistent with the dignity of a State institution, and should be scrupulously fitted and arranged to combine the essential requisites for the work for which they are designed. The noblest architecture in a democracy like ours, so long as its helpless and rapidly-increasing defectives are unprovided for, is not that which appeals to the sense of the grand or the beautiful. Splendid structures to gratify a cultivated taste, to excite admiration or wonder, to minister to sentiments of State pride, are infinitely less grand under such circumstances, and will prove far less useful and enduring, than plain, substantial, modest buildings, constructed " with the single purpose of adapting them to the uses for which they are designed." If these principles are held steadily in view by those to whom the State may confide the construction of the buildings needed, there will be no large departure from the estimates above named, unless some unlooked-for advance takes place in the cost of materials and labor.

OBJECTIONS NOTED.

There are two principal objections urged against the erection, at the present time, of institutions for the care and education of our defectives.

The one having the largest popular currency is that our unfortunates are already adequately cared for. While the obligation of the State to furnish the means of education to these afflicted classes is fully acknowledged, it is alleged that provision is made for them under our existing laws in suitable schools in other States. Unfortunately, this statement belongs to that class of illusory and obstructive propositions known as half-truths. The real state of the case is that while there are certainly not less than three hundred and fifty educable children in the State who would avail of institutions within our own bounds, only a few over one-third of that number are in reality enjoying the benefits of schools in other States. There

*

are numerous causes which conspire to produce this result, among which are the following:

1. The ignorance, weakness, and quick apprehensiveness of many parents, and the solicitude and affection of others contribute to prevent numbers of our defective children from being sent to institutions out of the State. It is felt that they are remote, comparatively difficult of access, crowded, not subject to the inspection of our own authorities, and non-accountable to them for possible abuses or mismanagement. No children are more tenderly loved by parents than these afflicted ones, and there are none for whom the mother, in especial, is under so constant a strain of solicitude and trembling anxiety. Doubtless, oftentimes this is morbid; but it is nevertheless a providential adjustment that motherly love should burn with a more fervid heat for those who most need a mother's watchful care and protection. Whatever its origin, and however sentimental it may be in its nature, it is, notwithstanding, a *fact* which *must* enter into our calculations and be credited with its due weight.

2. Numbers of parents are repelled from availing of the existing laws for the benefit of their defective children, because those laws are chiefly in the interests of the *indigent*. The very title of the law—"An act for the instruction and maintenance of *indigent* deaf and dumb," etc.—is repellant. Many who are in humble, straitened, limited or moderate circumstances are thus debarred from its advantages. They cannot truthfully describe themselves as " indigent;" and an honorable self-respect restrains them even from taking advantage of the provision by which the State offers to defray so much of the expenses of an institution as is beyond their means. The practical result is that our beneficiaries are principally derived from the indigent classes; which fact re-acts to give to institutions for defectives the injurious and unjust reputation of being "pauper establishments," and misleads parents into the criminal folly of refusing to have recourse to them for their educational and other advantages.

It is confidently believed that if the recommendation of the commissioners is accepted by the State, to make these institutions *free schools* for the education of all the defective children in the State who are within the educable ages, whether rich or poor, and without any humiliating conditions of admission, they will be eagerly availed of by the classes which are now experiencing the greatest deprivation and whose children are greater sufferers than those of any other class—namely, those who are wealthy, or whose means are limited or moderate. Nor only this, but it is the conviction of your commissioners that, in one year from the completion of the buildings and their readiness for the reception of pupils, they will be filled to the utmost capacity contemplated for them in the plans herewith presented.

The half-truths which proceed upon the presumption that our defective children are already adequately cared for in the schools of other States, are met by another consideration. Our children are only received on sufferance in many of these institutions, and our reliance on them may be painfully disappointed at any day. Already complaint has been made in the legislature of one of the States, whither our children are sent, that they need the room for their own unfortunates, who are crowded out by those from our State. The directors of the Pennsylvania Institution for the Deaf and Dumb, at which institution we have a number of children, have notified the State of Delaware to remove its deaf mutes; and the query is a pertinent one, "When will the turn of New Jersey come for a like notification?" In their last report, the directors of that institution expressed their regret that a large number of deaf mutes, residing in their own State, "were of necessity denied admission because the buildings are already taxed to the full extent of their capacity." Is it to be supposed that the people of Pennsylvania will long submit to such a condition of things, or that they will be patient under the exclusion of their own children for the benefit of ours, or that they will tax themselves for the erection of new buildings for our accommodation? It is scarcely reasonable to believe that they will do either of these things.

The other objection which is urged in favor of postponing for the present the erection of buildings for these unfortunates by the State of New Jersey, is a financial one. It is alleged that the expense would be greater than the revenues of the State will warrant, and that the necessity is not so great as to justify direct taxation. Without admitting the correctness of the assertion as to the necessity not justifying taxation, the commissioners fully recognize the force of facts. Undeniably, it is not desirable to exceed the revenues of the State, if it can be avoided. It is equally undeniable that a proposition to have recourse to direct taxation would be received with general and cordial disfavor.

The commissioners believe, however, that the buildings now most imperatively needed can be erected by the State without resorting to either of these unpalatable expedients. They are advised that there is now in the hands of the Riparian Commissioners, the notes of the Central Railroad Company of New Jersey, given in liquidation of riparian claims of the State, which notes, of $100,000 each, fall due respectively on April 1st, 1875; July 1st, 1875; and October 1st, 1875. By the act for the increase of the school fund, passed April 6th, 1871, it was enacted "that all moneys hereinafter received from the sales and rentals of the land under water belonging to this State, shall be paid over to the trustees of the school fund, and appropriated for the support of free public schools, and shall be held by them in trust for that purpose." The act further directs that the same shall "constitute a part of the permanent school fund of the State, and the interest thereof be applied to the support of public schools, in the mode which now is or hereafter may be directed by law, and to no other use or purpose whatever."

The commissioners respectfully suggest to your Excellency and the legislature the wisdom and propriety of the necessary legislation appropriating, before they are paid into the school fund and become a part of its permanent capital, the proceeds of these notes as they fall due, or as much of them as may be necessary, for the erection of an institution for the deaf and dumb, and of an institution for the feeble-minded, or one of them. Such legislation seems to be expedient and equitable, for the following reasons: The intention of the act of April 6th, 1871 was, generally, to further the cause of education ; in particular, through the medium of free public schools. While we are aware that by the "free public schools" referred to in that act, it was intended to designate those specifically so called in the "act to establish a system of public instruction" in this State ; and while we, therefore base no claim to the diversion which we suggest, upon the fact that the proposed institution for defectives will also most emphatically be "free public schools," we invite attention to the consideration that by such diversion no violence will be done to the motive which inspired the act of 1871, but that it is in harmony therewith. Should the proceeds of the notes above named be appropriated as the commissioners suggest, there will be merely a diversion of the amount from one form of education, or public instruction, to another. Moreover, the public schools, which last year received from all sources the munificent sum of $2,304,000, and which will doubtless receive at least as much more during the current year, will not be sensible of a diversion of funds which they never possessed. They are not suffering for the amount, and will be unconscious of its loss.

Whether the diversion that we suggest can be legally and equitably affected by a supplement to the act of 1871, is a question that we are not competent to deal with, and it is respectfully referred to the judgment of your Excellency and the legislature.

An allusion was made to the question which we have now raised, by your predecessor, Governor Parker, in his final message to the legislature. Speaking of the payment into the school fund of the proceeds of riparian grants and leases, he says: "The constitutional provision protecting that fund has been strictly obeyed. No part of the *principal* has been drawn therefrom, nor has any part of the interest been used except for school purposes. Although it is true that while the State is engaged in constructing large public buildings, the State fund needs more revenue, and that since the two mill tax has been levied the necessity of augmenting the school fund has not been so great, yet the law of 1871, above referred to, should not be disturbed. Should the legislature, however, think it wise to divert any of the riparian moneys hereafter to be received, from permanent investment in the school fund, such moneys should be used only for educational purposes or for the establishment of institutions germane thereto." Sharing these views, the commissioners respectfully invite an application of them by the legislature in the manner hereinbefore suggested, namely, for the establishment of institutions for defectives which shall be free public schools for the education and care of the deaf and dumb, the blind and the feeble-minded of New Jersey, for whose education there is no present provision within the limits or jurisdiction of the State.

ARGUMENTS ADDUCED.

There are several grave reasons for the establishment of these institutions in our State at the earliest practicable day, to which the commissioners invite the attention of the legislature.

It needs no lengthened exposition to show that every uneducated child, whether it be a defective or otherwise, is non-productive to the community, in the ratio of the density of his ignorance. Whoever is at the bottom of the educational scale contributes literally nothing to the material, intellectual, or moral welfare and prosperity of the society of which he is a unit; absolutely nothing but his impaired and misdirected (more often than well-directed) brute force to the wealth, or greatness, or perpetuity of a commonwealth or nation. Nor is this all. While the class to which he belongs adds nothing to the general welfare, it is the most fertile of all others in those aggravated forms of social evil which are the reproach of civilization; the most abundant of all in its supply of paupers, drunkards, incapables, and atrocious criminals, with the long legacy of evils, injuries and expenses, that follow in their train.

All that is true of the uneducated classes at large in these particulars is but a shadow of the truth as it respects uneducated defectives. These are not merely relatively, but absolutely unproductive; and, in addition, they are invariably a burthen—either to their parents or the State. By the nature of their infirmity they are infinitely more helpless to protect themselves, and infinitely more exposed to shameful outrages by the wicked, the inhuman, and the sensual than any others of the race, not excepting even the insane—outrages which degrade them to the level of the beasts, and which take their revenge upon the commonwealth for generations, for the degradation which it permitted and the neglect it suffered, by a penalty of cost in woe and money that cannot be estimated. Reflect, that one single outraged, betrayed, polluted female of our defectives who are uneducated, irresponsible, and incapable of self-protection, may become (and doubtless in the past such an one has become), the mother of a progeny that will cost the commonwealth in the machinery of almshouses, prisons, courts, etc., a sum that might educate a thousand to a level that would lift them out of an atmosphere of crime and degradation, into one of reason, conscience, intelligence, self-protection, and self-support. Most appositely illustrating the cost to a community of its neglect of its poor and unfortunate, is the now familiar statement recently made before the State Charities Aid Association of the State of New York, by Dr. Harris, of the city of New York, concerning the progeny of a woman in one of the counties of that State. It had been observed that the proportion of paupers to the whole population in that county was abnormal—being one in ten. A further investigation revealed that certain names constantly reappeared in the criminal and poor-house records of the county, which led to an inquiry that followed up the traces of those families and studied out their genealogies. The inquiry was pursued, in one case, over a period of six generations of vice, and ignorance, and misery and crime, with a result that was as astounding as it is full of warning and instruction. Says the *New York Times*, from which we copy a summary of Dr. Harris's statement, with some reflections of its own superadded: "Some seventy years ago a young girl named 'Margaret' was left adrift in one of these villages—it does not appear whether through the crime or misfortune of others. There was no almshouse in the place; but she was a subject of out-door relief, probably receiving occasionally food and clothing from the officials, but never educated, and never kindly sheltered in a home. She became the mother of a long race of criminals and paupers, and her progeny has cursed the county ever since. The county records show *two hundred* of her descendants who have been criminals. In one single generation of her unhappy line there were twenty children; of these, three died in infancy, and seventeen survived to maturity. Of the seventeen, nine served in the State prisons for high crimes an aggregate term of fifty years, while the others were frequent inmates of jails and penitentiaries and almshouses! Of the nine hundred descendants, through six generations, from this unhappy girl who was left on the village streets and abandoned in her childhood, a great number have been idiots, imbeciles, drunkards, lunatics, paupers, and prostitutes; but two hundred of the more vigorous are on record as criminals. This neglected little child has thus cost the county authorities, in the effects she has transmitted, hundreds of thousands of dollars in the expense and care of criminals and paupers, beside the untold damage she has inflicted on property and public morals. When we think of the multitude of wretched beings she has left upon the earth; of the suffering, degradation, ignorance, and crime that one child has thus transmitted; of the evil she has caused to thousands of innocent families,, and the loss to the community, we can all feebly appreciate the importance to the public of the care and education of a single pauper child." Any comment, evolving a teaching from the case of this unhappy girl, for the care and education of our superlatively helpless and exposed defectives, is needless. It conveys its own moral; and we should feel that any amplification for the benefit of the legislators of New Jersey would be an insult to their understanding and an imputation upon their enlightenment and humanity.

RESPECTING TRUSTEES, ETC.

If the legislature should conclude to act favorably upon the recommendations of the commissioners, and to authorize the erection of one or more institutions, it is respectfully suggested that, in conformity with the method that has been pursued and found to be advantageous in other States, a board of trustees should be appointed for each, two of whom should reside in the county wherein the institution is located, and a majority within a conveniently accessible distance of the same. In other States, it has also been found convenient and advantageous to divide the original trustees into three equal classes, to serve for two, four, and six years respectively, and to provide for filling the vacancies as they occur, by other trustees for the term of six years. By this means, the State will secure in the trustees, the presence of a majority who will be experienced in the duties and responsibilities of their position, and familiar with the details of their several institutions. Provision should also be made disallowing trustees to be pecuniarily interested in any contracts for buildings pertaining to the institution or institutions, or in furnishing supplies therefor; requiring the treasurer of the board of trustees to give suitable bonds; and empowering the trustees to appoint a competent superintendent, and other instructors and officers. Finally, it is suggested that the said trustees, or a special commission, be charged with the duty of drafting a law, to be submitted to a subsequent legislature, to cover all the necessities of the case with relation to the several institutions, and the admission of pupils thereto. Or, should the legislature prefer to perfect a law at the present session, we respectfully refer them to the act of the State of New York, entitled "An act defining the objects of the New York State Institution for the Blind," as a wise and comprehensive basis from which to frame a law that may be applied to all the defective classes. This act may be found, printed at length, in the report made to the legislature of 1874, by the commissioners on the deaf and dumb, blind, and feeble-minded, for that year. Copies of that report can be supplied by the undersigned commissioners.

SUMMARY.

The commissioners, in conclusion, present a summary of the several recommendations they offer to the consideration of the legislature for its action.

1. That the legislature accept the tract gratuitously offered to the State by the city of New Brunswick, as a site for an institution for the deaf and dumb; and that it take such action as will enable the people of that city to carry their generous proffer into effect.

2. That as soon as the present objects of the "Soldiers' Children's Home" shall have been accomplished, and its existence shall have terminated, the legislature apply the grounds and buildings appertaining to it to the uses of an institution for the blind, in conformity with the plans herewith submitted.

3. That the legislature appropriate the sum of $18,b00 for the purchase of the property at Bordentown, hereinbefore described, for the purposes of an institution for the feeble-minded.

4. That the legislature examine into the advisability and legality of an appropriation of the notes of the Central Railroad of New Jersey, herein more particularly described, now in the hands of the Riparian Commissioners, or so much of the proceeds thereof as may be necessary, for the erection of an institution for the deaf and dumb, and for an institution for the feeble-minded; and that, if the same may be legally done, the legislature enact a law applying the said notes, or so much of their proceeds as may be needed, for the erection of said institutions.

5. That the legislature appoint, or provide for the appointment of, a board of trustees for each of the institutions to be so established; and take steps for the drafting of a law to cover all the necessary provisions for the conduct, management, and control of said institutions, and regulate the admission of pupils thereto.

All of which is respectfully submitted.

Yours very truly,

CHARLES D. DESHLER,
JEREMIAH BAKER,
WILLIAM S. YARD,
CHARLES D. HENDRICKSON,
ELDRIDGE MIX,
RALPH P. GOWDY,
Commissioners.

February 10th, 1875.

CPSIA information can be obtained
at www.ICGtesting.com
Printed in the USA
LVHW021506261118
598291LV00012B/1268